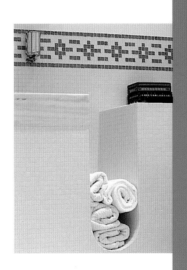

MAKING
THE MOST OF
BATHROOMS

MAKING
THE MOST OF
BATHROOMS

CATHERINE HAIG

RIZZOLI
NEW YORK

First published in the United States of America in 1996 by

Rizzoli International Publications, Inc.

300 Park Avenue South

New York, NY 10010

First published in Great Britain in 1996 by

Conran Octopus Limited

37 Shelton Street

London WC2H 9HN

ISBN 0-8478-1975-2

LC 96-67705

Commissioning Editor	Denny Hemming
Project Editor	Helen Ridge
Copy Editor	Tessa Clayton
Designer	Liz Hallam
Design Assistant	Amanda Lerwill
Picture Research	Claire Taylor, Clare Limpus
Production	Mano Mylvaganam
Illustrator	Sarah John

Printed in Hong Kong

CONTENTS

This stylish bathroom has two clearly defined roles – bathing, at left, and storage, at right – visually separated by the design of the floor tiles. The wavy black-and-white dividing line is echoed by the serpentine-fronted cupboards. These create a much greater feeling of space than a straight wall-to-wall arrangement and help to soften the rectilinear, galley-like shape of the room.

The circular basin, encased in the same wood as the cupboards, and the cast-iron bath with its ball-shaped feet continue the curvy theme. As the taps and mixer spout are wall-mounted centrally above the bath the bather can lie facing either end of the room and there are, accordingly, two niches in the tiled wall for soaps and shampoo.

INTRODUCTION

The past one hundred years have seen a remarkable revolution in bathing and bathrooms. A century ago, the once-weekly familial bath, taken in a tub laboriously filled by hand in front of the living-room fire, was gradually being superseded for the lucky few by the first Victorian and Edwardian bathrooms, complete with vast baths and substantial plumbing. As technology improved and demand increased, so bathroom fittings began to be mass-produced on a scale more suitable to the average-sized home. Today, thanks to sophisticated modern plumbing and design, most of us can enjoy a piping-hot bath simply at the turn of the tap, at any time of day or night.

These advances in design and technology mean that the modern bathroom is a much more flexible and personal room than ever before. At its most minimal, it can occupy remarkably little space, carved, for example, out of an existing bedroom or a redundant attic. At the opposite extreme, it can be one of the most luxurious rooms in the house, wholly dedicated to the comfort and wellbeing of the user. While single-room apartments require ingenuity to incorporate even the basic minimum of fittings, most houses today offer the option of one bathroom and an extra toilet and many have the extra space for an en suite bathroom, a separate shower room or a downstairs cloakroom.

Whether installing a brand-new bathroom or revamping an old one, initial planning is of vital importance. There has been a huge expansion in the range and variety of bathroom fittings available, all designed with maximum hygiene, comfort, practicality and convenience in mind. No longer is the bathroom seen as the poor relation in terms of design, and manufacturers are vying with one another to produce the most elegant, as well as the most comfortable and economical, bathroom suites on the market. For the purchaser, this excess of choice can be more than a little confusing and it is essential to know exactly what sort of fittings you require and whether they will be suitable for the intended location. Taking time to plan ahead, armed with tape measure and graph paper, can help to translate ideas into reality and to ensure that you really do end up with your perfect bathroom.

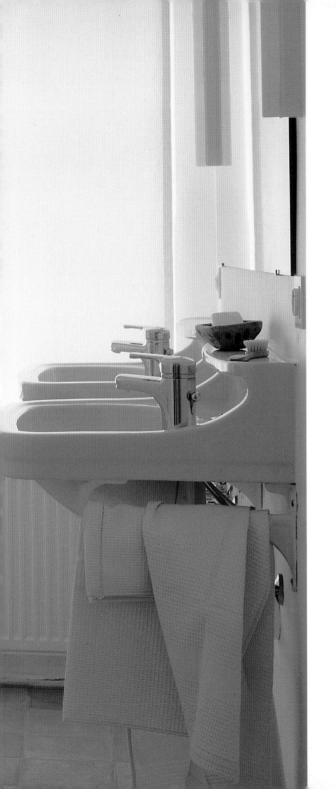

PLANNING

Planning a new bathroom can be a daunting prospect. Not only does it involve choosing the right fittings but it may also mean extending and, in some cases, completely reorganizing the existing plumbing in order to accommodate them. Whether you want to install a completely new bathroom or make improvements to an old one, there are still the same decisions to make and problems to overcome. The first step is to define the role and requirements of the new room; the rest will follow.

TAILOR-MADE

A bathroom must be tailored to personal
requirements and every plan will vary
according to the likes and dislikes of the
planner(s). This spacious bathroom
(previous page, left) is shared by a
couple. They opted for double basins,
centred against the wall at right, with
storage units, bath and toilet set against
the opposite wall. A low tiled wall
projects between the bath and toilet,
providing privacy for the latter as well
as completing the splashproof surround
for the bath. Storage takes the form of
simple, open shelves with plenty of
space for piles of towels and linen.

Others may prefer closed or concealed
storage space such as this built-in
ottoman with a hinged lid (previous
page, right). The space inside is ideal for
use as a laundry basket or for storing
towels, cleaning supplies and toilet
paper, and the ottoman doubles as a
seating area when closed.

Planning a bathroom involves more
than the positioning of the basic fixtures
such as the bath, basin, shower unit and
toilet; make sure your plan allows plenty
of floor and wall space for 'extras' such
as a towel rail, mirror and laundry
basket (right).

ASSESSING THE SPACE

Whether you are planning a brand-new bathroom or making improvements to an old one, taking a moment to think about the exact role of the room may save expensive mistakes later on. Ask yourself the following questions: Is the bathroom to be used by the whole family, just the children, a couple or a single person? Should it be en suite with the main bedroom? Is it for guest use only or will it serve the whole house? Will it require any special adaptations to suit the elderly or young children? Will it need to double up as a dressing room, exercise area or a laundry with facilities for washing and drying clothes?

The answers to these questions will determine almost every decision you make concerning the bathroom, from the choice of fittings to the choice of decoration. You may have always dreamed of having a super-powerful shower but if the other potential users of the bathroom are all under five years old, you may wish to think again. Similarly, a luxuriously carpeted room may be unbeatable in terms of comfort but it will certainly not give much pleasure or last very long if it is permanently soggy thanks to careless teenage bathers. The bathroom is a much-used room and both its design and decoration must be strictly tailored to suit its occupants and their requirements.

The next step is to establish whether the intended space can be plumbed. Take advice about local water and plumbing regulations; they vary from area to area and it is vital to understand their implications before you start. Secondly, unless your house is very new, the existing plumbing has probably 'evolved' over the years and it may be necessary to make changes so that the system can accommodate the new bathroom. It may be that your hot water tank is not large enough to cope with the extra demand. Existing pipework and plumbing may influence the siting of the bathroom itself and the positioning of the fittings within it: for example, it is much easier to connect a new toilet if it can be linked into an existing waste pipe.

Once the space has been allocated and the plumbing considered, begin to plan the layout of the bathroom. Use graph paper to map out the position of the fittings. Most bathroom catalogues include a sheet of graph paper for this purpose and some even provide line drawings to scale of toilets, basins, bidets, baths and so on. Cut them out and juggle them around to see how best to incorporate each piece. Don't forget to allow for access as well: you need enough space to get from one fitting to another and to use them in comfort; this is especially important if more than one person will be using the bathroom at any given time. Keep plumbing guidelines in mind: a toilet may be easiest to connect when sited against an outside wall; toilet and bidet should ideally be placed side by side; basin and bath water need to be channelled away in the same direction.

When choosing the fittings, keep your earlier definition of the bathroom in mind. If the room is to be used by the whole family, a separate shower unit might be preferable to a shower over the bath, as it would allow more than one person to wash at any time. Double basins are also worth considering. If space permits, install the toilet in a separate room to avoid delays at peak hours. Choose serviceable, splashproof materials for floors and walls and invest in a large mirror, a laundry basket and plenty of shelving.

- Take professional advice before planning a bathroom. Take into account local water regulations, existing plumbing facilities and the construction of your house.
- Draw out the area on graph paper and study how best to divide up the bathroom for different tasks. Look at the options of various 'dividers' such as double or sliding doors, archways, curtains and changes in floor level.
- Ensure that space is available not only to accommodate your chosen fittings but also to move them into position. For example, a heavy cast-iron bath is awkward to manoeuvre. If the staircase is too narrow, could the bath be winched up and brought in through a window? Will the floor take the strain once the bath is full of water?
- Be realistic about the possibility of future plumbing problems and allow for access to potential trouble spots such as the shower pump and boxed-in toilet cisterns. Fit removable panels instead of sealing these utilities in behind fixed walls.
- Build in utilities such as good heating, ventilation and lighting. They are vital to ensure that the bathroom both looks good and works efficiently.

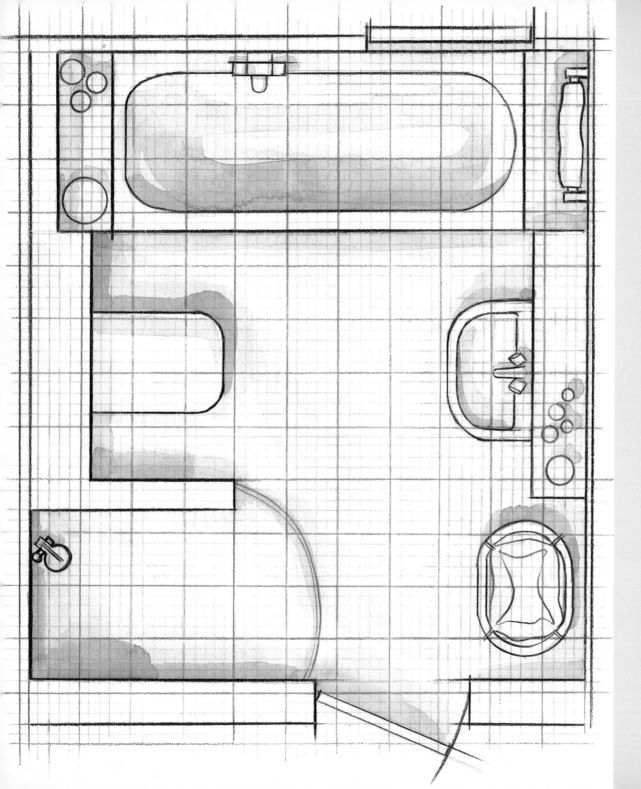

DRAWN TO SCALE

When planning a bathroom it can help to map out the fittings to scale on graph paper first. This floor plan (left) relates to the bathroom shown at right and on the previous page. Note the division of space: the bath runs almost the whole length of one wall, with tiled 'extensions' at each end filling in the gaps. The toilet and basin face each other while the shower is partially separated from the rest of the room by a full-height projecting wall. Basin and toilet are wall-hung and, in each case, a false wall has been built out from the original bathroom wall to accommodate the necessary pipework and plumbing. Tiled and painted to match the rest of the room, these projections are hardly noticeable but give the room a much neater, more streamlined finish. The basin wall has also created a handy alcove for the laundry basket.

Shelf space around the bath, basin and shower was planned before work began. The false wall behind the basin created an instant shelf (see previous page) and the recessed wall above was lined with mirror. The areas at both ends of the bath were tiled to match the walls and a niche was carved out of the shower wall for soap and shampoo bottles (right).

If young children are going to be the main users of the bathroom, choose fittings that will accommodate short legs: a wall-hung basin, for instance, that can be set at an appropriate height; a toilet with a low-level cistern and a lever that is easy to reach; a bath with a relatively low side and a flat, non-slip base; a shower with a sliding shower head rather than a fixed one and, if possible, a thermostatic safety control to prevent small hands suddenly causing a surge of scalding water. Many an accidental bang on the head can be avoided if you wall-mount the bath taps and mixer spout; this will also keep the controls out of reach.

Make sure that at least one cupboard is fitted with a secure lock to keep medicines and cleaning agents out of harm's way. Buy a rubber suction mat for the bottom of the bath and a large, absorbent bath mat for the floor outside. Flooring generally should be non-slip even when wet and this applies especially to the areas by the bath, the shower, the basin and the toilet. If you fit a lock on the inside of the bathroom door, position it well out of your children's reach.

Some of these guidelines apply for the elderly as well, such as a shower with a thermostatic safety control and non-slip flooring. A shower door that opens inwards or slides will reduce the likelihood of water dripping on to the floor, making it slippery. The bath should similarly have a flat, non-slip base but in this case a high side is a help rather than a hindrance, allowing access to the bath without too much bending or straining. Some sort of bath chair on a swing arm may be required for the very infirm; position the bath to accommodate the fixings. Choose taps or levers that are easy to turn and add helpful 'extras' such as grip rails in the bath and shower and judiciously placed seats.

A bathroom plan should also incorporate changes of floor level, if appropriate. Here, the shower area is defined by a lowered floor (above) which, together with the partition wall, retains most of the fall of water, allowing the shower to be used at the same time as the rest of the bathroom. The flooring throughout the room runs to skirting-board height and the join with the tiles is well sealed to prevent any water seeping through. The wall-hung toilet and basin (above and above left) stand clear of the floor, making it an easy-to-clean surface. Both bath and basin are fitted with streamlined modern taps, and a white ladder-rack towel rail (seen on page 10) makes good use of the otherwise redundant space at one end of the bath.

UTILITIES

A well-designed bathroom does not just function well, it is also warm, cosy and inviting to use. Make sure you take time at the planning stage to think beyond the basic necessities, such as fittings and fixtures, to elements such as lighting, heating and ventilation. These are easy to install at the time of building, but expensive and disruptive to alter or add to later on.

Water and electricity are a lethal combination and it is vital that the accommodation of these utilities is carefully and safely planned. Some of the bathrooms shown in the pages of this book do feature electric sockets, but in many countries safety rules and regulations do not allow them, or specify their location. In the United Kingdom, for instance, there must be no socket outlet within the bathroom at all, unless it is a special low-voltage shaver unit, and any light fitting or other electrical supply must be worked by means of a pull-cord if it is within reach of the shower or the bath. If in any doubt at all, seek expert advice.

The bathroom tends to be used most in the early morning and late at night and good lighting is of paramount importance. Normal ceiling lights and wall lights are permitted in bathrooms, provided they are correctly wired in and safety guidelines are adhered to. A permitted alternative to pull-cords is a switch on the wall outside the bathroom door. If the ceiling is very low or the light is to be positioned over the bath or shower, pendent lights and ordinary inset spotlights are not recommended. Instead, choose from a wide range of specially designed bathroom lights, including sealed bathroom spotlights which are designed to function in a wet, steamy atmosphere.

SAFETY FIRST

When space is restricted, it may be necessary to extend the bathroom's role to include washing – and sometimes drying – clothes and bed linen. Appliances can be installed within bathrooms but they should be positioned well out of reach of the bath and shower and must be safely wired. In this bathroom (left and right), for reasons of safety and aesthetics, the machines have been concealed behind sliding mirrored doors. When the doors are closed, the mirror serves to increase the feeling of space within the bathroom, creating no break in the all-white scheme; when open, they offer easy access to the appliances and, with the doors sliding back one behind the other, take up minimal space.

Washing machines and tumble dryers tend to generate a lot of condensation, and if you plan to install such appliances you should make sure the bathroom is well ventilated. As this room has no windows, the owners have installed ventilation ducts, which also provide a casing for the inset spotlighting.

It can be hard to decide where to position the lights until you have actually started to use the room but, as a general rule, over-light rather than under-light. Taking a light source out later on is far less expensive and disruptive than adding one after all the decoration has been completed. Place a light near the bath to allow for reading or shaving; light the mirror over the basin, positioning the fittings to throw light on to you rather than the mirror in order to reduce glare, and ensuring that the light or lights are sufficiently wide to illuminate the sides as well as the front of your face. Pay particular attention to dark corners or recesses; a judiciously placed light focused on an object or picture can transform a dreary corner into a feature of the room. If the room contains cupboards, fit lights inside that come on automatically when the doors are opened; this is one example of a highly practical and effective 'extra' that is easy to install while the bathroom is undergoing construction, but awkward later on.

Heating and ventilation are also of prime importance. A heated towel rail will provide a modicum of warmth but most of this will be absorbed by the towels. A bathroom radiator or a radiator and towel rail combined can help to increase the heat, as can underfloor heating if installed during construction. Don't forget that towel rails warmed by the heating system will not function in the summer when the heating is turned off. Even in hot weather, it is still much nicer to have warm, dry towels so either choose a rail that can be connected to the hot-water system or substitute an electric one.

It is not essential to have a window in a bathroom but, given the hot, steamy atmosphere and the inevitable condensation, it is vital to have adequate ventilation. Building regulations require that an extractor fan be fitted in the absence of an openable window and it is most usual for the fan to work in conjunction with the light. Fans can be programmed to stay on for some twenty minutes or so after the light has been switched off.

Hair dryers, fan heaters and similar electrical equipment are not permitted in bathrooms but larger appliances such as washing machines or wall heaters can be installed, provided that they are permanently wired into sealed sockets. They must not be positioned within reach of anyone using water, so should be well out of the way of the bath or shower.

Telephones are permitted in bathrooms but again, for reasons of safety, it is not advisable to have an ordinary telephone socket in the room. The effects of steam and condensation on the telephone itself must also be taken into account. One solution is to have a telephone on an extra-long lead in the next-door room or to install a portable, cordless model which can be carried in and out of the bathroom.

ON SCREENS

As well as the siting of fixtures and fittings, planning a bathroom also involves making sure that there is adequate space for washing and bathing, for storage, and for any additional activities such as dressing or exercising. In a small room there is less room for manoeuvring, but in a larger room, the different areas need to be carefully planned and defined.

Screens are useful tools for creating both a decorative and a practical division of space. In this spacious, high-ceilinged bathroom (right), a triple-panelled screen serves to create a cosy area around the bath and acts as a visual divide between the two ends of the room. Made of wood, it has been painted to tone in with the decoration of the room. In addition, at the far end of the room long curtains suspended from a wooden pole hide the contents of the shelving system from view.

Floor-to-ceiling panels screen this bathroom (right) from its adjoining bedroom. The panels have been cleverly engineered to slide within grooves in the ceiling and are easily opened and closed. Twin deep-sided sinks with matching taps, mirrors and shelves below can be seen to either side of the bathroom, with the shower cubicle behind, but toilet and bidet remain discreetly hidden even when the doors are open. When closed, the panels camouflage the bathroom completely, blending in with the matching panels at right which screen off storage in the bedroom. Deliberately designed to be free of all detail, including handles, the panels complement the spare, minimalist theme of the decoration.

DIVIDING SPACE

Maximizing the potential use of any bathroom depends on an appropriate division of space within the room itself as well as the way in which it is connected to the rest of the house. Again, this involves considering the list of questions at the beginning of this chapter: you can only decide how best to allocate space once you are sure of who and what the bathroom will be for.

Division of space involves defining the boundaries of the bathroom. You may wish to carve up an existing bedroom, or create an extra room in the attic. You might choose to extend a room by taking in all or part of an adjoining room or passage. Or you might find extra space under the stairs or in a hallway, for example, for a toilet or shower room. Within the bathroom, it involves allocating space for the different items that may be required: for example, a shower fitted over a bath, or a bath and separate, self-contained shower unit; double or single basins; storage; a dressing-room area; or utilities such as washing machines and tumble dryers.

The dividing lines may be either decorative or structural. Breaking up the space may simply be a case of installing a screen or different flooring or tiling to indicate a change of use within the bathroom, or it may involve physically separating a bathroom from its en suite bedroom. Whatever the situation – and it will be different in every case – the division of space must be decided at the planning stage. Walls, doorways, floor levels, positioning of fittings and fixtures are all still fluid at this point and with the help of a tape measure, a pencil and a sheet of graph paper, it is possible to experiment before making any unalterable decisions.

Within the bathroom itself, divisions of space can be decorative and/or practical. A raised floor around the bath might separate that area from the rest of the room and, if tiled to match the surrounding walls, might also create a waterproof 'platform' within an otherwise non-waterproof floor. Screens are economical options; they can be fixed, as in sliding doors or panels, or freestanding, either painted or decorated, or fabric-covered for a softer effect. In its freestanding form, a panelled screen can be placed around the toilet, for example, to increase privacy, or near the entrance to the room to cut down on draughts, as well as providing a useful place to hang towels or robes.

Separating the toilet from the rest of the room or, if space permits, installing one toilet within the bathroom and another elsewhere in the house, can greatly increase

MAXIMIZING POTENTIAL

Partitioning space is an easy way to increase the potential use of a bathroom without having to divide it into separate rooms. In this room (above and right), the bathroom area is divided from the dressing area beyond by partition walls which visually separate the two, though access remains open. In addition, the toilet, bath and shower, ranged along one wall, are separated by a trio of tiled projecting walls. These serve to give privacy to the toilet area and to create a splashproof cubicle for the shower. They also enclose the bath and provide enough space to hang a towel rail.

Note how changes in flooring can be used further to define different areas: here, the toilet area is tiled throughout in the same black border tiles used to edge the main floor-covering.

the potential of a bathroom used by more than one person. A standard toilet and a wall-mounted basin can be fitted into a surprisingly small space, requiring only about 140cm x 90cm (55in x 36in) in total. Alternatively, a toilet can be screened or partially screened from the main area of the bathroom by a partition wall – with or without a door. Even a low-level partition wall, rising to about 90cm (36in) in height, would serve to increase privacy, as well as doubling up as a useful shelf to house toilet paper and accessories.

If your shower is to be open-plan with the rest of the room, some sort of screen or partition may be appropriate to keep the basin and toilet area dry. Even if the whole room is tiled and therefore entirely splashproof, it may still serve to increase the potential use of the bathroom if both shower and basin can be used at any one time without both users getting soaked.

Dual-purpose bathrooms

Dual-purpose bathrooms may work better if the two areas are divided or semi-divided. In a bathroom-cum-dressing-room, for example, the storage area for clothes would benefit from being separated in some way from the moisture and condensation of the main bathing area. This might involve fitting a standard cupboard with hinged or sliding doors or creating a large, walk-in closet. It might simply be a case of hanging a curtain which would cut down on dust and add a decorative touch.

In certain countries, such as the United Kingdom, regulations dictate that appliances such as washing machines have to be positioned out of reach of both bath and shower, and the installation of some sort of screen or divider would enhance the safety factor as well as conceal

these less-than-decorative items from the rest of the bathroom. Sliding doors are a space-saving option, while double doors look attractive and can be designed to fold back flat for ease of access. A word of caution about boxing-in any appliances, especially washing machines or tumble dryers: take care to ensure that there is sufficient ventilation and that installation instructions are correctly followed. A tumble dryer, in particular, generates a great deal of condensation and most models require a vent leading to an outside wall.

One possible drawback of dividing space within the bathroom is that each individual area may have to be independently lit, but powerful angled spotlights and clever use of mirrors can help overcome the problem.

OPEN OR CLOSED?

The division of space between a bedroom and its en suite bathroom can be as formal or informal as you like. These two rooms (right) are virtually one, separated only by a wide curtain-lined arch. The striped ticking fabric is tied back to reveal the cast-iron bath on its elegant grey slate plinth. The shape of the splashback echoes the archway, and brass swan-neck taps complement the brass bedstead. Wide oak boards run, almost uninterrupted, throughout the two areas.

By contrast, the illustration (far right) shows how a bathroom can be carved out of a bedroom, the two separated for reasons of logistics by conventional walls and a sliding door. Every inch of wall space within the bathroom is needed to accommodate just the basic fittings and there is no room for decorative manoeuvre. As the entrance to the bedroom has virtually been reduced to a passage, cupboards occupy the remaining space, freeing up the rest of the room for bed, armchair, table or bookcase as required.

EN SUITE

Once experienced, an en suite bathroom is a luxury that it is hard to give up. Even if you think you have no spare room in the house, it may still be a possibility, given careful planning and clever division of space. If your children have

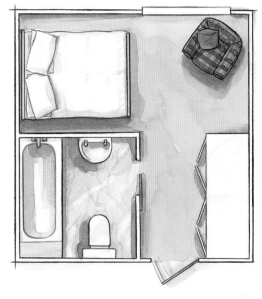

grown up and left home, then a bathroom adjacent to the main bedroom, supplemented by a smaller shower and toilet elsewhere, would be a practical arrangement. If your house has sufficient bedrooms, then it may pay dividends to convert one into a bathroom and knock through the adjoining wall. If an existing bedroom is large enough, there may be space to fit a bathroom within it, either screening or semi-screening off the two areas or simply leaving them open-plan.

However the two are arranged, an en suite bathroom is designed first and foremost to be used in conjunction with an adjoining bedroom and the division of space should reflect this. A conventional doorway is the most usual 'divider' but if space is at a premium and a door takes up too much room – particularly if you feel that it will always be left open anyway – then there are alternatives.

Depending on the positioning of the two rooms, an archway between the two can create a decorative visual divide. An arch is always a graceful architectural feature in a room and, large or small, it allows easy access while keeping the bathroom at a discreet distance. It can be hung with a curtain for a decorative effect or for extra privacy, or left elegantly open.

A difference in floor levels can also create a visual divide between a bedroom and bathroom. Perhaps combined with a doorway or archway, steps either down or up help to define the separate areas.

ONE ROOM OR TWO?

An en suite bedroom and bathroom should ideally be planned as one unit, taking into account access between the two, the view from one to the other and a sense of continuity in terms of decoration.

Given the size and proportions of this room (left), it seemed unnecessary to divide the space at all and the bathroom has been largely incorporated into the bedroom scheme. Toilet and bidet are housed in another room but the decorative period-style bath and basin blend easily with the white Lloyd Loom chair and lace-covered bed. French windows ensure ample ventilation and the polished wooden floor is suitable for both bedroom and bathroom use.

An archway and a change of floor level serve to separate this bedroom and bathroom (right) while matching paintwork and floor-covering unify the two spaces. The classic black-and-white theme of the bedroom is carried through to the bathroom, echoed in the smart black bath and the thick, white towels.

Double doors can provide a flexible alternative. They allow the two rooms to be closed off from each other completely when shut, and yet virtually made one when open. They would be particularly appropriate in cases where an en suite bathroom has another access and might, on occasions, be used by people other than the occupants of the adjoining bedroom.

An en suite bedroom and bathroom should be planned in conjunction. Not only should they look good together, complementing each other in decorative terms, but they should work well together. Depending on the positioning of the two rooms, the less-than-decorative items such as the toilet and bidet should be discreetly placed out of sight from the bedroom. If they cannot be hidden, then folding wooden screens, either painted or decorated with decoupage or fabric, a curtained canopy, an opaque glass screen or a simple semi-partition wall can all be brought into play. Another ploy is to focus attention elsewhere, making a decorative feature of the bath or basin.

Continue the style of decoration through from one room to the other. The bathroom need not be a replica of the bedroom but should echo the same themes. Use matching fabric at the windows or complement the wallpaper in one room with a fabric in the same design in the other, and run the same floor-covering throughout both rooms, if possible, for an added sense of continuity.

One final consideration: particular attention should be given to heating en suite bathrooms, especially if the bathing area is not sectioned off from the bedroom. Large rooms are difficult to heat evenly, and you might want to consider additional heating near the bath to ward off post-bathing chills.

Conventional storage units can be adapted to contain fixtures and fittings in bathrooms where, for reasons of privacy or aesthetics, it is necessary to screen off certain elements. The key element of this peaceful, contemplative retreat (below right) is the large marble soaking tub which stands squarely in the middle of the room. Plain white panels line the walls, cocooning the bather and screening off the other areas of the bathroom. Hidden behind this all-white wall are the toilet and bidet, storage space and the V-shaped marble basin with its simple spout and chrome extending mirror just visible here. All clutter and activity is contained within and nothing intrudes upon the soothing atmosphere of the bathing area.

MADE TO MEASURE

Once all the bathroom fittings and fixtures are in place you may find there is little room left for free-standing cupboards and shelving, so it is vital that storage is considered at the planning stage. Returning to the graph-paper floor plan of your bathroom, assess the available space. Remember that no elements, except perhaps the windows, need be constant. Building a false wall a few feet out from a real one might create an ample walk-in closet. Alternatively, build out to either side of the basin or the bath, creating a decorative alcove (which could be mirror-lined) and providing twin storage units. Use the space above and below the fittings: set the basins into cupboards and utilize the otherwise wasted area above the bath with a row of shelves or a towel rail. Modular shelving units need not necessarily stand against a wall; projecting at right angles, they can also serve as decorative room dividers.

Built-in storage units are a good way to make use of every available inch of space. Made to measure, they can be fitted into awkward alcoves or under sloping attic ceilings. A row of floor-to-ceiling cupboards will give a room a streamlined finish, as well as disguising less decorative elements such as the hot water tank or cluttered shelves.

BEHIND CLOSED DOORS

Twin storage units have been built out from the wall to either side of the basin in this sunny, well-lit bathroom (right). The 'cupboard' on the right houses a toilet; the other provides ample space for a shower. The shower's interior is fully tiled and the unit has a conventional shower door, which provides a better seal than the exterior door. Linked by the pedimented mirror above the basin, the two units add an architectural note to the room, creating a decorative feature out of necessity. For good measure, the design of the doors neatly echoes the shutters at the window and the panels on the bath.

STYLE

With the practicalities of planning under way, it is time to turn to the more creative side of bathroom design. The style of your bathroom requires careful consideration as it will dictate your choice of fittings and decoration. To help you build up a picture of the effect you want to create, keep a file of ideas: jot down points of interest from other people's bathrooms, and tear out magazine articles for inspiration. But most important of all, allow yourself to dream a little.

Creating the style and atmosphere of a bathroom need not necessarily be complicated or expensive. Tiled in a bold chequerboard design, this cream-and-turquoise bathroom (previous page, left) combines great style with simplicity and practicality. Bright Mediterranean colours lift the tiling out of the ordinary and, together with the hand-finished effect of the tiles themselves, create the feeling of being inside an Italian *palazzo* or an ancient Roman bathhouse. The broken run of cornice above one end of the bath enhances the atmosphere. All that needs to be added are soft white towels and plenty of hot, scented water.

Sometimes the fittings themselves can dictate the style of a bathroom. A feature as striking as this beautiful antique blue-and-cream basin with its original brass taps (previous page, right) would lend instant charm and character and establish the look of the rest of the room: plain cream walls and the simplest of curtain treatments would be all that would be required to show it off to its best advantage.

COUNTRY

Whether it is designed to complement a rose-covered cottage or as an escapist retreat from urban reality, the country look always works well in a bathroom setting. Easily created, involving inexpensive materials and simple techniques, the effect is pretty, fresh and appealing.

The classic country look is perhaps best associated with sprigged floral wallpapers and flowery fabrics, which, together with accessories such as bunches of dried flowers, are readily available and have a timeless appeal. The country-style bathroom, ceiling included, is often entirely decorated with floral wallpaper, complemented by wall-hung flower-patterned plates or prints. A window curtain decorated with spring blooms might be matched with a basin frill in the same material or, for an original touch, a curtained canopy around the bath. The scheme can also be extended to fixtures and fittings: Victorian basins and toilets were often decorated with fresh blue floral designs and though the originals are much sought after and difficult to obtain, reproduction models are easily available.

Variations on the gingham theme, with one-colour or multi-colour checks, work just as well in a country-style bathroom as in a classic country kitchen. Try simple and uncomplicated curtain treatments with gingham fabric hung from a painted wooden pole or tied with bows on to a wrought-iron one.

The country style implies a certain nostalgia and fittings usually follow a traditional theme: large, old-fashioned washstands with brass legs; cast-iron baths with ball-and-claw feet; high-level toilet cisterns worked by pull-chains; wooden toilet seats and towel rails.

Walls and floors should have a rustic feel. Plain white paint, evoking traditional whitewash, creates a crisp, fresh background while natural matting, painted or stained floorboards or terracotta tiles might cover the floor. Stencilling allows a decorative motif, perhaps taken from the curtain fabric, to be repeated on walls, cupboard doors, floors and the sides of the bath. Cupboards and shelves are in rustic pine – sanded and sealed rather than painted – with doors and windows to match, evoking the wooden beams of old country cottages. Wicker baskets, filled with soaps and potpourri, add an inviting touch.

RURAL RETREATS

Rustic wooden beams and whitewashed walls evoke the spirit of the country in the two bathrooms shown here. The brickwork above this basin (left) has been left unplastered and the white-painted shutters provide a little privacy during the daytime when the checked curtains are open. White walls in this spacious, airy bathroom (right) provide a fresh, light foil to the row of maplewood cupboards. These, in turn, complement the beamed ceiling, with the natural grain, texture and colour variation of the wood playing their own part in the decoration.

In the larger room, the bath takes centre stage. Unusually, it stands on a pair of wooden brackets, rather than cast-iron legs, and still has its original lever-operated brass plug.

Pictures and accessories play almost as great a role as fittings and decoration in creating a traditional-style bathroom. An old document, mounted and framed, hangs above the bath (left), while prints, photographs and memorabilia cover almost every remaining inch of wall space. A portrait (right) is flanked by two framed panels of antique blue-and-white tiles. Collections of silhouettes are grouped to either side and a large gilt-framed mirror hung over the basin makes a striking statement.

TRADITIONAL

Recent years have seen a great revival in 'traditional' bathrooms that evoke the stately, rather masculine style of the Edwardian era, when bathrooms were sumptuously – if rather cumbersomely – decorated. Original fittings have come back into vogue and architectural salvage firms are flourishing as home decorators scour the country for old brass taps, basins, roll-top baths and commodes; these are invariably beautiful to look at but they need careful restoration to function properly and a lot of time and effort is required to keep them looking good. Luckily for all those who have little time to seek out the genuine article, manufacturers have been quick to respond to demand and most bathroom showrooms and catalogues now offer well-designed and authentic-looking traditional ranges.

The centrepiece of most traditional-style bathrooms is a large, cast-iron roll-top tub with decorative ball-and-claw feet and polished brass taps. Alternatively, a standard bath can be set into a marble surround with side panels of glossy, dark-stained wood, evoking the mahogany fixtures of times gone by. Whatever its size and shape, however, the bath is always a cast-iron one; these rooms look back to the days well before the invention of acrylic.

Basins are usually capacious affairs, either freestanding complete with matching pedestal, or built into a marble or mahogany surround. Taps are pillar-style with handles rather than modern levers or mixer controls. Toilets have

wooden seats and high-level cisterns with pull-chains or are concealed within converted Edwardian commode chairs with hinged wickerwork seats.

Decoration tends towards the masculine with rich, deep colours, plenty of dark polished wood, heavy rugs on the floor and elaborate curtaining. *Faux* panelling, either throughout the room or just below a dado rail (chair rail), can be painted in, while wallpapers inspired by archive print collections can lend an authentic touch. Window treatments in faded, tea-stained linens, old chintzes, silks and damasks are hung on heavy wooden poles with decorative finials, or enhanced by pelmets finished with lavish fringes and tassels.

These bathrooms have a warm and lived-in feel. Ornaments, photographs and books reflecting the owner's interests are arranged on every possible surface and, together with glass-fronted prints and paintings hung on every wall, would look equally at home in a study or dressing room. Furniture features prominently. A large mahogany chest of drawers, topped with a dressing-table mirror and perhaps a set of silver-backed brushes, provides storage for linen or clothes. Space permitting, there might also be a wardrobe, a linen press or an upholstered ottoman.

Accessories such as a gleaming brass bath rack, a shaving brush and bowl, a collection of glass bottles for scent, bath oils and aftershaves, and monogrammed linen hand towels and bath sheets hung on a chunky chrome heated towel rail continue the old-fashioned theme. Comfort, above all else, was the ultimate aim of the Edwardian bathroom and, thanks to modern heating and plumbing, today's reproductions far exceed those original expectations.

In deliberately not conforming to any particular style, shabby chic has become a style all of its own. Fixtures in these bathrooms are unmatched and unfitted but every piece is unusual and beautiful in its own right.

An antique blue-and-white bowl (near right) has been converted to a basin and sunk into a work surface, and is filled by means of two taps similar only in style and finish. The pipework has not been chased into the wall but is clearly visible.

The eye is drawn to the splendid bath, the vast open fireplace and the array of decorative objects in this characterful bathroom (centre right) and the general air of dilapidation merely enhances the atmosphere. The scale model of a toilet, complete with minuscule toilet-paper holder, provides an eccentric focal point, while an elegant, if tattered, armchair invites rest and relaxation.

In the pale blue bathroom (far right), an old-fashioned enamel sink is backed by a slab of grey-veined marble and flanked by cupboards painted with an appropriately distressed finish.

SHABBY CHIC

An expression which has only recently entered the home decorator's vocabulary, 'shabby chic' describes that peculiar mix of style and dilapidation which, in the right hands, can be a truly magical formula for decorating success. It takes a practised eye, a confident touch and, preferably, a crumbling French *château* or Italian *palazzo* to achieve its full glory, but there are elements which are adaptable to bathrooms on a more modest scale.

The shabby-chic bathroom is the absolute antithesis of the fitted bathroom. No elements are built in, nothing matches, pipework and plumbing are flaunted rather than disguised and fittings are either old or, at the very least, unusual. The focus is often one particular element – a magnificent cast-iron bath, a splendid wardrobe or a beautiful mirror – beside which everything else in the room pales into insignificance.

Fittings have an individual touch. They may be new but seem curious and original, as if they have been picked up at random from auctions or antique shops. This is not the look for those who have just invested in a brand-new bathroom suite; it is more appropriate for those who have inherited a bathroom and need to replace one or two items but cannot find anything that matches the existing scheme. Variety here is definitely the spice of life, and differences should be exploited rather than concealed.

Unusual pieces of furniture or decorative items are employed in unexpected ways. A china bowl, sunk into a washstand, makes an eye-catching basin. An antique jug might be used to hold toothbrushes and toothpaste. A panel of old tiles, set into the wall, could make a

characterful splashback above the bath. Objects are used and valued for their intrinsic beauty rather than their conformity to an overall decorative scheme.

When it comes to decoration, the theme is the same: nothing is conspicuously new. Walls are either left in their natural state or subtly colour-washed and irregularities in the plasterwork are left untouched rather than disguised. Woodwork can be left unpainted or rubbed down to allow the grain of the wood or the layers of paint underneath to show through. Rather than conventional blinds or curtains, window treatments might include an old velvet throw or an oriental hanging loosely draped from a pole or tacked to the window frame and swagged to one side. Using the original shutters, if your house still has them, or placing a Victorian decoupage screen in front of the window might prove an apt alternative. Upholstery is visibly ancient, with worn tapestries or washed-out chintzes covering a chair or

chaise longue. A magnificent but tattered Persian rug may take pride of place on the floor, but the boards underneath show their age and imperfections. A gilt-framed mirror is propped rather than hung above the basin while an unframed old master hangs above the bath.

The overall effect is one of gracefully faded grandeur and elegance, with every item in the room telling an intriguing and nostalgic story. But do not be deceived: the taps may not match but they produce gallons of hot water just as effectively as their brand-new counterparts and the old-fashioned radiator pumps out heat. Shabby chic definitely does not mean spartan chic.

MODERN

Most new bathrooms are modern as opposed to antique in style, but the truly modern bathroom goes one step further. Here are state-of-the-art fittings, encased in sleek, sophisticated materials such as chrome, stainless steel, sand-blasted or acid-etched glass. The emphasis is on design with a capital 'D' and the effects are invariably dramatic.

Modern bathrooms tend to be monochromatic, with clean lines and sharp contrasts. Walls are white, either painted or tiled, or may be sheathed in panels of glass or steel. The floor may be lined in studded rubber or crisply chequered linoleum in black and white or a combination of bold primary colours. Windows are uncluttered by curtains but could be shaded by metallic slatted blinds or custom-designed glass panels.

Bathroom fittings are striking to look at but always supremely functional. Many modern furniture designers have turned their hand to bathroom design, reinterpreting the standard shapes of basins, baths and taps in dramatic and highly individual ways. Some of these pieces are unique, designed to order; others are more accessible and can be found at good bathroom showrooms.

Alternatively, standard fittings can be given a contemporary feel by clever use of the materials around them. Side panels of brushed steel and up-to-the-minute mixer taps with high-tech controls would transform the most basic bath, while a standard under-counter basin could be sunk into a glass worktop for a streamlined effect. Inset low-voltage lighting adds drama to any room and even the smallest details, such as chrome cupboard door handles, can contribute to the overall effect.

STATE OF THE ART

Contemporary bathrooms make full use of high-tech materials and state-of-the-art lighting. They push back the boundaries and experiment with new techniques and combinations.

Polished stainless steel and sand-blasted glass are the key elements of this ultra-modern bathroom (left). The bath appears almost suspended above the floor due to its reflective stainless-steel plinth and to the sand-blasted glass side and end panels which are back-lit with fluorescent lighting. The polished stainless-steel panel above the bath creates another play on space, reflecting the wall-mounted taps and mixer spout.

Fluid curves counter the strong lines. There is a tubular towel rack (seen reflected in the panel) and the washstand is almost spherical with a sand-blasted glass top and a curved bowl. A bolster-style headrest adds a touch of luxury.

TALE OF THE UNEXPECTED

A fantastic bathroom may be supremely luxurious, just plain enormous or downright eccentric but it always contains that element of the unexpected – the 'gasp' factor. Stepping into this bathroom (right) with its vista of the garden is a case in point. Not only is the bather virtually at one with nature – note the extensive 'daylighting' set into the timbered ceiling – but this is also the most luxurious of personal health spas. A huge whirlpool tub with cushioned mats and pillows at either side, a massage table and (safety regulations permitting) a television screen allow for moments of quiet relaxation, while the more energetic can make use of the wall bars, weights and exercise bicycle.

The stone-and-white bathroom (far right) is a more contemplative retreat. Here objects of art and antiquity surround the bathers as they recline in the vast double bath with dual headrests and mosaic surround. A decorative glass panel on wheels can be used to screen off the view through the ceiling-high French windows and an alternative vista is offered by the television screen encased (together with a music system) in the cupboard at right.

FANTASY

Fantasy bathrooms are literally the stuff of dreams for most of us but, with a little thought and a touch of self-indulgence, any bathroom can become a sybaritic retreat.

Fantasy bathrooms are spacious, comfortable and luxuriously decorated and equipped, with good heating, an abundant supply of hot water, a large bath, possibly fitted with a whirlpool, and deep-cushioned seating. They are rooms that indulge the mind as well as the body, and can double up as exercise rooms, health spas, media rooms or studies. In some countries, such as the United Kingdom, safety regulations preclude having hi-fi systems or televisions in bathrooms, but equipment outside the room can be connected to speakers within so the bather can relax to a favourite concerto. Similarly, a portable telephone or one with a long lead allows for conversations in the bath. Most average-sized bathrooms could incorporate a set of wall bars or an exercise bicycle, while a whirlpool bath need not take up any more space than an ordinary one.

DECORATION

A practical bathroom can still be a
stylish one; in fact, decorating the
bathroom often allows the imagination
greater scope than the more public
rooms of the house. Colour and pattern
can be introduced in paint, fabric or
tiles, or simply used to accent a
monochrome scheme through accessories
such as towels, soap dishes, pictures or
plates. A favourite decorative object
such as a piece of china or a special
mirror is often an effective – and very
personal – starting point.

Three rectangular windows, punched out of the wall, allow the view from this seaside bathroom (previous page, left) to become part of the decoration. Wild in winter and calm in summer, the drama and movement of the seascape is uncluttered by curtains, blinds or architraves. The only adornment is the trio of tiles which lend height and interest to the windows and link with the tiled basin surround. The walls and vaulted ceiling are rough-plastered and painted throughout in a deep Mediterranean blue to echo and frame the view outside.

A completely different 'all-over' effect is achieved in this small windowless bathroom (previous page, right), lined with tongue-and-groove boarding. A shelf at basin height divides the boards used below from the slightly narrower ones above, a device which increases the feeling of height in the room. The walls, cupboards and mirror surround are all painted the same shade of blue, which unifies the scheme and allows features such as the moulded mirror to stand out.

WALLS AND CEILINGS

The earliest Victorian and Edwardian bathrooms were either wonderfully grand, marble-walled affairs or smaller, more modest rooms bedecked with flowery wallpaper and gathered curtains. For today's bathrooms, however, the array of choices is vast and choosing the right finish can be more than a little daunting.

Start with an analysis of the room itself. The bathroom, for all its sybaritic connotations, is essentially a functional room and it is important that you take this into account when planning your decorative scheme. For example, wallpaper might be an appropriate choice for a spacious, well-ventilated room with windows, but a less practical option for a small, windowless shower-cum-toilet that is likely to generate a lot of condensation.

Damp causes problems, particularly in old houses, and it is therefore vital to protect vulnerable areas of the bathroom. Even if you do not intend to tile the whole room, consider the areas around the bath, basin and shower and remember that a shower head placed over the bath will require a much more extensive splashback than a bath with conventional taps. Alternative solutions to tiling include glass, mirror or clear Perspex (Plexiglas) screens.

Give yourself a realistic budget. Bathrooms are expensive rooms to fit and often there is little left over for decoration. If costs have to be cut, look at other ways to achieve the effect you want. Enliven plain tiles by using a coloured grout or by laying them diagonally; paint existing tiles a more appealing colour; paste inexpensive prints straight onto the wall with wallpaper paste instead of spending money on frames, and don't dismiss the idea of

WAYS WITH WALLS

Tiny mosaic tiles are used in this distinctive bathroom (far left, above) to create a decorative and practical wall finish around the basin and bath. Based on a cream-coloured ground, the pattern incorporates the charcoal grey of the cupboards and mirror frame. Note how the design depends not only on the colour but the positioning of the tiles to create a fluid, freehand effect.

At the opposite extreme, this shower room (left) uses tiles and colour on a grand scale. Large squares in a palette of earthy tones line the walls, the chequerboard effect enhanced by dark grey grouting. Pipework for the shower is concealed, with just the controls, the shower head and soap dish visible.

Tongue-and-groove panelling creates an alternative and effective form of splashback and bath surround in this simple, uncluttered bathroom (far left, below). The boards rise to chest height to protect the walls from spray from the hand-held shower. Painted pale aqua blue, using an oil-based, water-resistant paint, they give way to plain white above. Wooden hooks provide storage for towels and other necessities.

a plain white bathroom out of hand – sometimes less is more. Finally, take the size of the room into account. Turning a tiny bathroom into a palatial marble-lined 'spa' might be within your budget whereas creating the same effect in a larger room would prove extremely costly.

Paint is a wonderfully versatile medium and can play both a practical and a highly decorative role in the bathroom. Water-based paints are traditionally used on walls and ceilings alike; the latest ranges of heritage paints have added another dimension to the standard colour charts, and are ideal for decorating rooms with a period feel. Oil-based paints include gloss and eggshell, the former producing a very high gloss finish, the latter a more subtle, silky sheen. Both are suitable for woodwork and are wipeable, which is always an advantage in family bathrooms. For rooms with poor ventilation which might be especially prone to unsightly damp and mould, some manufacturers are now producing special fungicidal bathroom paints.

Applying a specialist paint finish is a relatively easy way to give walls added colour and interest. The simplest forms are the techniques of sponging, ragging and stippling; more complicated are effects such as marbling or wood-graining. Traditionally, the coloured glaze is applied onto an eggshell ground, using sponges, cloth or special brushes, but the latest innovations on the market are 'instant' paint-effect kits with rollers, which create similar results. Seal with matt varnish for a very practical, hard-wearing finish.

For a paint-free alternative, seal bare plaster with varnish, adding a dash of colour if desired, to exploit rather than conceal any imperfections in the wall.

MARINE THEMES

A treasured shell collection has been put to good use in this bathroom on a seashore theme (left). Against a background of glazed aquamarine walls, with a natural-looking, almost 'rubbed' paint effect, shells and starfish motifs are ranged above the mirror and tiled bath surround. Painted white and applied at random, they also appear on the tiles themselves, making a striking decorative feature out of a plain white, inexpensively tiled wall.

The oval mirror is framed with shells of different shapes and sizes, some set inside-out to vary the effect and to reveal the delicate colour variations of the shells' undersides. Reflected in the glass, a wooden shelf displays the overflow of the collection.

Shells and starfish are popular themes for the bathroom and, in the absence of the real thing, look out for fabrics, wallpapers and tiles with seaside motifs; stencil walls and ceilings with a variety of marine life; hang framed shell or fish prints on the walls, and choose towels and other accessories with a seashore theme.

LABOUR OF LOVE

The free-form wall design of this shower cubicle (left) was painstakingly created from fragments of tiles. You may baulk at the idea of buying perfectly good tiles only to break them into pieces, but here the final result is totally unique and eye-catching. The original shapes and colours of the tiles can be seen in the unbroken squares around the shower tray – white, black, brown and light blue – but the finished design owes nothing to straight lines or right angles. The fluid curves and scrolls are abstract and elegant and create a dramatic feature out of functional necessity.

Wallpaper is not usually recommended for bathrooms because damp and condensation can cause it to peel away. However, given a spacious room with plenty of ventilation, wallpaper is certainly an option to consider and it works particularly well in traditional-style bathrooms. Vinyl wallpapers are specially designed for bathroom use and, though formerly rather heavy and 'plasticky', some are now almost indistinguishable from ordinary papers and come in a good selection of colours and designs. Wallpaper borders can be pasted around the top of the walls at cornice level to finish a painted wall, or placed at dado-rail (chair-rail) height to divide, for example, a painted area below from wallpaper above. Use up the remainder of the roll to create imaginative 'frames' around mirrors or prints, or to add depth and interest to plain, unmoulded cupboard doors.

Tiling is an art form in itself and is a practical and decorative way of creating a waterproof surface around showers, basins and baths. Tiles come in a variety of materials including ceramic (machine- or hand-made), terracotta, marble, granite and slate, and in every imaginable colour and design. Vary the theme by using small mosaic tiles to build up a pattern or motif, or by using contrasting borders or insets.

A BATHER'S-EYE VIEW

The large, old-fashioned chrome shower head (below right) was the inspiration for this painted ceiling, which replicates the pattern and design of the shower holes. The perfect circle near the top of the wall gradually stretches and elongates as it crosses the ceiling, creating a subtle play on space.

Bath-time travellers can lie back and plot their next expedition with the map of the world pasted on to the ceiling above the bath (centre right). Artfully 'held up' by a gilded cherub in the corner, it is an amusing modern variant on the ornate painted ceilings of old stately homes, and just as entertaining.

Mirrored panels play a dual role in the bathroom. First, a mirror of some shape or size is invariably necessary for shaving, applying make-up and so on; second, thanks to mirror's reflective quality and play on light, it acts as a 'space enlarger', making even the smallest bathroom appear more spacious. A mirror can be an attractive and practical option for a dingy bath or basin alcove.

Panelling walls in wood or metal has added advantages: the panels can be used to conceal any unsightly pipework and to visually unify an awkwardly shaped room. Edwardian bathrooms often featured dark polished mahogany panels to dado- or to picture-rail (chair- or plate-rail) height, and the same technique can be reinterpreted today. Tongue-and-groove, which can be either painted or stained, is an inexpensive option;

alternatives include panels of stripped pine, limed oak, painted wood, or stainless steel for a streamlined look.

Ceilings are a neglected area when it comes to decoration and are usually painted unobtrusive white or cream. However, the bathroom ceiling does come into view when you are lying back in the bath and repays a little time and effort. Consider taking your chosen paint finish up and over the ceiling for a cosy, cocooning effect. Alternatively, create a real 'sky' by sponging soft clouds in white against a pale blue backdrop, or stencilling gold stars over a deep blue ground. If your budget allows, commission a painted mural or consult one of the specialist vinyl suppliers who use computer-aided design to create intricate patterns for floors: the same techniques can equally well be applied to ceilings.

AIMING HIGH

Ceilings are the Cinderellas of the
decorating world, almost always
overlooked when planning the
decoration of a room and invariably
painted in muted, plain colours. Here,
however, the ceiling echoes the brilliant
yellow of the cast-iron bathtub and is
very much part of the vibrant decorative
scheme (right). Partnered by pink walls
and reflected in the mirrored mosaic
detail in the tiles, the colour is warm and
bright and acts visually to lower the
ceiling, counterbalancing the tall,
narrow proportions of the room.
Accessories such as the towels and bath
mat play on the colourful theme,
ensuring a sun-filled room even on the
dreariest of winter days.

FLOORS

Bathroom flooring must be practical but it need not necessarily be cold or clinical. Just as with walls and ceilings, the starting point must be to assess the future use of the bathroom. If it is to be used by children or old people, the floor must not become slippery when wet. If it is en suite to a bedroom and therefore only for the use of one or two people, comfort might come higher up the list of priorities. Or if it is likely to be subjected to a lot of 'traffic' and wear and tear, durability and ease of cleaning will be of paramount importance. When making a choice, estimate both for the cost of buying and for the cost of laying the floor; sometimes the cheaper floor-coverings can be more expensive to fit, and vice versa.

Top of the list for comfort is carpet. Ordinary carpet is not usually recommended for bathrooms as it can become smelly and rot if continually subject to damp. However, in cases where comfort is more important than practicality, and where splashes and spillage can be contained to a minimum, this is a risk worth taking. A useful alternative is bathroom-quality carpet, which is rubber-backed and made of cotton or synthetic materials that are more resistant to a damp atmosphere.

Natural floor-coverings such as seagrass, jute, sisal and coir are also vulnerable to damp but most varieties are rubber-backed and, with care, can be used. Some natural materials are rather scratchy and therefore unsuitable for bare feet, so test them for feel as well as appearance. Good-quality bath mats, particularly if used over old-fashioned cork boards, can help considerably towards keeping any floor-covering dry.

Vinyl and linoleum are traditional bathroom floorings which have recently come back into favour and are available in an excellent variety of colours and patterns. Both are relatively cheap to buy and to lay (depending on the state of the original floor) and extremely easy to maintain. Contract-quality vinyls are completely non-slip and would be appropriate in bathrooms with open showers. Cork tiles, another traditional option, are similarly easy to clean, appealing to look at and comfortable on the feet. They do, however, need to be properly laid and sealed in order to function well. A more

NATURAL CHOICES

Natural materials make good choices for bathroom floor-coverings. Traditional terracotta tiles lend warmth and character to this all-white bathroom (left). They provide a firm base for the roll-top bath with its cast-iron legs and are proof against any accidental splashes or spray from the hand-held shower. The drain hole shown in the foreground makes cleaning less of a chore; water can be sluiced under the bath and storage units, then wiped up with a mop.

Seagrass matting is rubber-backed and can be laid with or without underlay. A smooth base is important and a layer of hardboard underneath to cover uneven floorboards is often a prerequisite. The natural textures and tones of seagrass complement the decoration of this colour-coordinated bathroom (right) with its polished plaster bath and basin surrounds and translucent cotton curtains. A cotton bath mat protects the matting beside the bath while the pair of stainless-steel basins are set well back to minimize spillage. Chunky soaps and a collection of wooden boxes continue the natural theme while the sculpture makes a striking focal point in the corner of the room.

THE BARE ESSENTIALS

Sometimes in our haste to select a floor-covering, we neglect the obvious choice – the existing floorboards. To make a satisfactory floor, particularly in a bathroom where bare feet are the order of the day, the boards have to be in reasonable condition. Replace any rotten boards and re-fix loose ones before sanding and sealing for a smooth and lasting finish.

In this old-fashioned bathroom (right) the floorboards have been given a decorative twist with a black-and-white painted chequerboard design. While the grain of the wood is still clearly evident, the effect is a play on the classic vinyl bathroom floor and works well with the old-fashioned roll-top bath and wrought-iron washstand. By contrast, the wooden panelling and Shaker-style pegs have been given a pale limed finish.

modern look can be achieved with rubberized studded flooring which is available in a variety of textures and colours. Though totally waterproof and practical, it can be awkward to clean if the studs are too prominent.

Marble, ceramic and terracotta tiles are all highly appropriate for bathrooms in that they are water-resistant. If very highly glazed, they may be slippery when wet, but non-glazed, non-slip and textured tiles are all available. A tiled floor can be cold on the feet and care should be taken when planning the heating of the bathroom to counter this; underfloor heating is one possible solution. When laying new tiles on floors (or walls), try to ensure that grouting is flush with the surface of the tiles; insufficient or chipped grouting creates the perfect haven for dirt and germs.

A useful detail for any bathroom with a tiled or vinyl floor that needs regular cleaning is a drain hole. This need not take centre stage but can be discreetly concealed in a corner, and even if it is not possible to slope the floor towards it, it makes washing a great deal easier, as well as taking care of any accidental spillage from the bath, basin or shower.

Finally, many houses have wooden floorboards which, if in reasonable condition, can be suitable as a bathroom floor. The boards need to be sanded down and then polished or painted – stencilling is a particularly decorative option – before being sealed. Add colourful cotton rugs for extra comfort in front of the basin or the bath. In the absence of old floorboards, consider laying a new wooden floor. Warm and comfortable on the feet, wood can be stained to any shade and is certainly one of the most durable and timeless materials.

The floor in this light, airy bathroom (above) was given the simplest possible treatment. The original boards were painted in plain white gloss, echoing the white stencilled designs on the turquoise walls, and topped with colourful cotton rugs. The floor catches the light that streams in through the window and bounces off the mirrored panel on the wardrobe.

LIGHT AND SHADE

Privacy is important in the bathroom, but there are alternatives to the ubiquitous net curtain. The windows in this all-white bathroom (right) are screened by simple white cotton Roman blinds which provide privacy while allowing sunlight to stream into the room. Their completely plain, unfussy design does not detract from the ornate detail of the tiles, which are the chief decorative focus of the room.

Internal shutters such as the ones in this bathroom (centre right) allow the bather to see yet not be seen. Light filters through the openwork pattern, casting ever-changing shadows on the walls. Recalling the latticework screens of the Moroccan *hamman*, the shutters lend a tantalizing air of mysticism to this otherwise functional modern bathroom.

An ugly view from a bathroom window can be successfully screened from sight by the use of a decorative glass panel (far right). Opaque glass alternates with lustrous blue to create a striking feature out of a formerly unprepossessing window. Good artificial lighting and the mirrored alcove help to compensate for the lack of natural light.

WINDOWS

Bathroom window treatments depend as much on what is outside the window as on the interior scheme. Urban houses may look out onto blank walls or neighbours' windows, both of which it might be preferable to screen off. A country bathroom, on the other hand, might open onto a marvellous vista with no other house in sight, and in this case privacy would not be a major consideration.

Ensuring privacy often means designing one form of screening for the day and one for the night. A voile curtain is effective in daylight but, at night, with the light behind

it, the bather is completely visible from outside. Conventional window treatments such as blinds or curtains are one solution; another, particularly if the view is poor, is a fixed screen of some sort – a wooden lattice, perhaps, or a decorative opaque- or coloured-glass panel.

Often used at night or early in the morning, the bathroom is always equipped with artificial light – many bathrooms are completely windowless. Hence, window treatments need not be constrained by the desire to maximize daylight. Use it and enjoy it if it is there but do not be afraid to screen it, either by a fixed panel as described above or perhaps by draping a curtain across the window or hanging a blind trimmed with a deep fringe.

Blinds are particularly practical for bathrooms, as they can be rolled up and kept well out of the way of damp floors and work surfaces. Roller blinds, either plain or made up in the laminated fabric of your choice, are one of the most basic forms. Roman blinds are equally simple, hanging flat against the window when down and pulling up into neat 'accordion' pleats. Pull-up or gathered blinds give a more decorative effect, and can be finished with a contrasting frill or pleated edging.

Even the simplest curtains can add great style to a bathroom. Gathered muslin, looped over a pole and held back at either side of the window with large bows, can add a touch of softness to the most functional of rooms; calico and ticking are inexpensive alternatives, while sprigged floral patterns add old-fashioned charm. It is also worth remembering that the original function of curtains was to exclude draughts and, in an house without the benefit of double glazing, thickly lined and interlined curtains might make the difference between a cosy bath and a chilly one.

Though the chrome finish of the details such as the towel ring and taps gives this bathroom (above) a sense of unity, the main decorative focus is the large circular mirror, complete with a useful magnifying mirror on a swing arm.

A few carefully chosen accessories can help create a restful and relaxing environment. This folding stool (right, above) provides a place to sit but is light enough to be easily moved to gain access to the cupboards behind, while towels are kept within easy reach on the chrome rail above. While some would consider a set of bathroom scales a necessity rather than a decorative accessory, this particular model also looks stylish.

ACCESSORIES

Bathroom accessories range from the purely practical to the purely decorative and run the whole gamut in between. In few other rooms do functional elements contribute so much to the decoration, with even mundane items such as soaps, towels and bath mats playing an important role.

When choosing your bathroom accessories, space and storage are two criteria to be considered. Space, or the lack of it, will limit choices as to what can be displayed and how. Some bathrooms barely have room for the minimum daily requirements, others can be used to display favourite collections of china or pictures. Make the most of the space available: a shelf at picture-rail (plate-rail) height is a decorative way to display objects while keeping them clear of water and out of the children's reach; a wall cabinet makes a perfect high-level base for a hand-painted plate, a china jug or an arrangement of dried flowers; a boxed-in toilet cistern becomes a useful shelf for soaps and bottles of scent and bath oil.

Objects in daily use need to be accessible, hence the use of open shelves, bath racks, towel rails and toilet-roll holders. Positioning needs to be practical: towels should be easy to reach from both shower and bath, if possible. Alternatively, double up and have two towel rails. There might be space at one end of the bath to keep shampoo, extra soap, bath oils and loofahs, as well as plants or decorative china.

Start with essentials. Bath towels, hand towels, face cloths, robes, a stool or chair and a bath mat can all be colour-coordinated with your scheme, but do not forget

the more mundane items such as the toilet-roll holder, toilet brush, towel rail or ring, hooks for bathrobes, a shelf or cabinet for medicines, toothbrushes and so on. Bathroom cabinets come in a selection of woods as well as chrome, brass, nickel, gold plate or plastic (white and coloured). A mirror, either framed or unframed, is another essential, and can be cut to size. Bevel the edges of an unframed mirror for a smarter finish.

Next, consider 'extras' which might both ease the running of your bathroom and contribute to its overall look: a bath rack, available in a variety of metal finishes

USEFUL EXTRAS

Accessories should be tailored to your requirements. In this bathroom (right, above) the accessories are more than purely decorative objects: note the folding table positioned so that the bather can still enjoy a drink while relaxing in the tub, the wooden floor mat by the basin – a warmer option for bare feet than chilly ceramic tiles – and the laundry basket with wheels allowing for easy manoeuvrability.

Chrome accessories work particularly well with bold colours. Here, the laundry basket, bath rack and table are all finished in chrome, while the soap dish, toothbrush holder, mirror and towels are in bright primary hues, taking their cue from the smartly patterned yellow-and-white tiled floor.

For bath-time bookworms, a chrome bath rack (right, below) is the ultimate luxury, keeping reading material well out of harm's way and still providing plenty of space for face cloths and soaps.

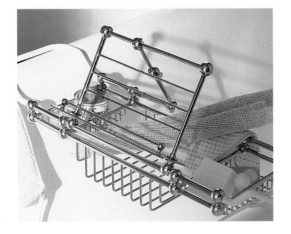

and woods; soap holders, either fixed to the wall or in the form of attractive china dishes or large shells; a shower rack; a laundry basket.

Even the smallest object can lend character or colour. Soaps and bath oils look decorative if artfully arranged. Toilet paper can be stored in a wicker basket or a large porcelain bowl. Toothbrushes can be kept in fine china, coloured glass or brightly patterned plastic cups. And nothing gives a bathroom greater character than a collection of favourite objects: a montage of photographs, clipped under glass; old certificates; inexpensive paintings and prints; shells, starfish, pebbles – anything goes.

LET THERE BE LIGHT

Bathrooms often require a combination of general and task lighting, the former casting a diffused glow over the whole room, the latter targeting certain areas. In this bathroom (right) the inset bathroom spotlights provide the general light while the row of vertical lamps

above the basin cast the task lighting needed for shaving or applying make-up.

The natural light that streams through the window of this cloakroom (above) is supplemented by the task lighting cast by the wall-mounted lamp. The wrought-iron sconce complements the ornate shell-shaped basin and swan's-head tap.

MIRROR, MIRROR

Mirror is an essential requirement in every bathroom and its reflective qualities can be used to enhance the room's lighting, as illustrated by the two bathrooms shown at right. The mirrored panel above the basin (right) visually doubles the effect of the three exposed light bulbs and their smart chrome fixings, bouncing the light back into the room. White tiles on the walls and the floor and accessories in crisp red-and-white add to the overall feeling of brightness. In the all-white room (far right), a pair of powerful inset spotlights provide task lighting above the basin but are also sufficient to light the whole room, including the shower area at the far end, thanks to the mirror which extends right across the alcove. A skylight provides additional light by day.

LIGHTING

Nothing is worse than a dingy bathroom and, given that this is a room that is most likely to be used in the early morning and late at night, a dark, gloomy atmosphere can only be avoided by well-planned, effective artificial lighting.

The main areas to target are the basin, where activities such as shaving can be disastrous without adequate light, and, to a lesser extent, the bath – particularly if you enjoy a leisurely soak with a good book. Depending on the size and shape of the room, choose between ceiling lights and wall lights or use a combination of the two.

Hanging lights can be decorative but are often impractical in a bathroom, especially if ceilings are low. Water and electricity are a dangerous combination and for reasons of safety and space it is better to opt for inset spotlights which fit flush to the ceiling. These do require adequate space between the ceiling and the floor (or roof) above, however, so check that your ceiling is suitable before you buy. Special bathroom spotlights, where the bulb is sealed into the unit to protect against splashes, are available for areas such as shower cubicles or low-ceilinged bath alcoves.

Don't forget that lighting also has a decorative role to play. Theatrical spotlights inset around the basin mirror make a feature of that area as well as providing an excellent source of light. Alternatively, for a different effect, an attractive, old-fashioned mirror can be enhanced by a pair of traditional lamps with coloured shades, set on wall-mounted sconces.

FITTINGS

Whatever the style and decoration of your bathroom, there are certain elements that are constants in every scheme: the bath, basin, toilet, shower, bidet and storage units. You may not require all of them but making the right choices is vital. Most bathroom fittings, if properly installed and cared for, will last many years and a mistake will be expensive and time-consuming to put right. Arming yourself with a few facts before you buy will help you to choose what is right for you and your home.

Taps, together with plug, chain and
'waste' (the technical term for the plug
hole and overflow) are often expensive
'extras' additional to the cost of baths
and basins and it is important to choose
designs that are appropriate and
function well with your choice of
fittings. The taps are wall-mounted in
this streamlined modern bathroom
(previous page, left), with a single
swivel-arm mixer spout feeding into
each of the twin stainless-steel basins.
All plumbing is concealed behind the
wall and in the units below the custom-
made glass work surface. There is ample
storage space both within these
cupboards and in the rectangular niches
in the wall, to leave the basins and work
surface completely clear and
uncluttered. Uplighters set into the top
of the cupboards cast a translucent glow
upwards through the glass.

Wall-mounted above the bath
(previous page, right), one set of taps
controls the flow of water to both the
bath and the shower. The bold, square
design of the taps is matched by the
chunky spout and chrome grip handle.
The shower has a hose long enough to be
used for hair-washing in the bath as well
as conventional showering.

BATHS

Traditionally made of enamel-lined cast iron, today's baths also come in steel, acrylic and new composite synthetic materials. Price may be a deciding factor in determining your choice but bear in mind that a cheap bath may not offer the best value for money in the long run.

Cast iron is still popular for traditional bath designs, and is strong, hygienic and exceptionally durable. Steel is a cheaper and lighter alternative; it, too, wears well but, like cast iron, has the disadvantage of being cold to the touch.

Moulded acrylic baths are warmer and come in a variety of colours but are not nearly as strong as metal baths and are more liable to scratch. Reinforced with fibreglass and mounted on a steel frame, they are light and easy to install. Look for a bath with a relatively thick layer of acrylic and a firm, well-designed casing; it is unnerving to step into a bath that 'gives' with your weight. Check especially around the curves of the bath where the acrylic may be thinnest and where the bath will be under most strain. Proper installation is also important to ensure that the bath is correctly supported and to safeguard against leakage.

TAKE THE PLUNGE

Most of us opt for metal or synthetic baths, but there are alternatives. Taking its cue from oriental soaking tubs, this bath (left) is made of wood. Extra deep, it can be used as a plunge pool for a refreshing dip after exercise or a sauna, or the bather can relax and float, in semi-suspension, in warm water up to the neck. The slatted seat is an optional extra and the chrome spout was specially designed to reach from the wall over the rim of the bath. Also available in more conventional materials, compact, deep baths are useful for small spaces.

REST AND RELAXATION

This curvaceous oval bath (left) is carved from a single piece of marble. As there are no taps or waste attachments to dictate which way to lie, the bather can either look outwards through the window at right (not visible) or gaze inwards at the surrounding monochrome space. Cool, restful and uncluttered, the room is devoid of any architectural or decorative details, cocooning the bather and allowing his mind as well as his body to be rested and refreshed.

The bath is filled by means of a floor-standing mixer spout which curves elegantly over the rim of the bath and is controlled by means of taps semi-concealed in the wall behind.

BACK TO BASICS

This stainless-steel bath (right) illustrates the concept of the metal bath at its most literal level. Devoid of panelling or enamel, the metal reveals its streamlined, reflective qualities to the full, making a striking feature in this marble-lined bathroom. The gleaming surface is easy to keep clean and, though cold to the touch initially, warms up quickly and is more heat-retentive than conventional cast iron.

The bath was designed to fit precisely into the alcove and the shower spray and taps have been wall-mounted accordingly. The high-level porthole window echoes the metallic theme and accessories are neatly contained in a net hung on the wall and in a glass storage jar.

HIGH AND LOW

As well as being panelled, baths can be raised on legs or, alternatively, sunk into the floor. A platform, running along two sides of this bathroom (right), creates a built-in surround for the spacious sunken cast-iron tub. A conventional bath in the same position would have cut into the deep sash window; given that there was sufficient space below floor level, this arrangement provided the ideal solution.

The ornamental ball-and-claw legs of a traditional cast-iron tub can be painted to match the body of the bath as shown here (far right) or given a contrasting colour. This Edwardian-style tub looks just as much at home in this sleek, spare setting as it would in a period room, its curved lines offset by the terracotta floor, white tiles and floor-to-ceiling glazed doors. The shower area is defined simply by a recessed floor and, on warm days, is literally open to the elements.

Relatively new to the market are baths made from composite synthetic materials developed and designed specifically for bath manufacture. Thicker and more rigid than acrylic, these materials are easily moulded, long-lasting and repairable. Baths made from synthetic composites keep the heat in well – six times longer than acrylic and twelve times longer than cast-iron baths – and are resistant to knocks and scratches. Their disadvantage is that they are comparatively expensive.

Baths can either be freestanding, as in the traditional cast-iron roll-top tub with ornamental legs, or panelled. Standard baths are usually panelled but matching side and end panels are generally not included in the price of the bath. Most baths are fitted into corners but if you decide to centre the bath against a wall, giving access from both sides, do not forget to budget for an additional side panel.

Bath sizes do vary, so it might be worth stretching out in a few different ones in the showroom before you buy.

Deciding factors should also include: lower sides if the bath is to be used by children but higher sides for the elderly so that they do not have to bend down very far if leaning on the side for support; a non-slip, flat base if there is to be a shower over the bath; a handle on one or both sides if required; tap holes positioned close enough together or far enough apart for the taps of your choice; the width of the bath (the larger the bath the more hot water it will require and if your supply is limited a narrower or contoured bath is a more economical option), and the possibility of fitting extra 'luxuries' such as whirlpool spas with jets of water which are particularly relaxing after hard exercise, as well as helpful in alleviating muscle stiffness or pain.

Before jettisoning your old cast-iron bath, consider restoration. Re-enamelling is not a long-term solution but the process of polishing the existing enamel to smooth out roughness or stains is very effective and can bring an old bath back to remarkable new life.

SHOWERS

Whether to bathe or to shower may still be the subject of debate but most modern bathrooms can, with a little planning, offer both options. The days when a feeble trickle of lukewarm water passed off as a shower are long gone and booster pumps and powerful shower heads have done much to restore the shower's image. On average, a shower uses one-fifth of the water of a bath and is a much quicker – and, some say, more hygienic – way to get clean.

Showers either draw on the hot and cold water tanks of the house, mixing the water to the required temperature, or are supplied direct from the rising cold-water mains, heating the water as required by means of a wall-mounted electric or gas-fired heater. If the first option appeals, it is essential that you consult a plumber first. Problems can occur if taps are turned on or toilets are flushed while the shower is on, causing the cold water supply to be diverted and making the shower suddenly too hot. The flow of water from the tank to the shower head is another factor to bear in mind as this will determine the pressure of water. A booster pump may be required. A shower supplied from the cold-water mains may be a less expensive and disruptive option, but for safety reasons, the gas- or electric-fired heater should be fitted by a professional.

Most modern showers are thermostatically controlled, avoiding sudden, potentially dangerous surges of too-hot water. Shower heads vary enormously; some have adjustable sprays allowing for both invigorating jets and a relaxing soft rinse. Fixed shower heads are neat and compact but detachable handsets are flexible and can be used at low level to wash hair or rinse out the shower.

If the shower is to be positioned over the bath, some sort of waterproof screen will be necessary. Panels of clear safety glass or toughened plastic, either fixed or hinged, are effective; a shower curtain is a relatively cheap alternative and is easy to install. The walls around the bath will also need to be splashproof up to shower height.

Shower trays for self-contained shower units come in various forms of vitreous china, acrylic, composite synthetic materials and enamelled steel. Sizes vary and rectangular and triangular forms are also available; if you are intending to tile the walls around it, check that the join between tray and tile can be properly sealed to prevent leakage.

Shower doors can be hinged like conventional doors, or can pivot, slide or fold back; these latter options can be useful in cramped bathrooms where there might be little room for a shower door that opens outwards.

TILE STYLE

Whether your shower is contained within a cubicle, positioned over a bath or 'open-plan', the walls around it need to be splashproof. A practical and relatively inexpensive option is to tile the area to shower height, ensuring that the grouting is waterproof. Plain white tiles line this shower (far left), including the recessed niches carved out of the wall for soap and shaving kit. The shower itself is a particularly compact model with all pipework concealed neatly behind the tiled wall.

The shower area in this bathroom (centre left) is open-plan, and walls and floor alike are tiled with terracotta squares. Triangular marble slabs provide shelf space and the shower fitting combines a slide rail and a hose for complete flexibility.

The curved casing of this enclosed shower (left) is designed to retain as much water as possible, the position of the shower head (not visible) directing the spray away from the deliberately narrow opening. Lined inside with white mosaic tiles and painted outside to match the walls, it makes an unusual feature in this attic bathroom.

GLASS WORKS

Positioning the shower over the bath necessitates a waterproof screen as well as surround. Standard shower curtains are available ready-made in washable and wipeable materials. Use plastic or rust-proof hooks and fixings.

The two bathrooms shown here illustrate the use of fixed or hinged panels. The screen of glass blocks (right) provides a semi-opaque divider, allowing the bold tiling behind the bath to show through and retaining the fall of water at the shower end of the bath.

By contrast, the bath (centre right) is completely contained behind a four-panel glass-and-chrome screen, creating in effect an extra-large shower cubicle. The two central sections fold back and the clear glazing allows light from the window into the room.

TOILETS AND BIDETS

Most toilets and bidets are made from vitreous china, a form of clay which is fired at a very high temperature and glazed to create a durable and hygienic surface. There are numerous different designs to choose from, some looking to the past, others more streamlined and modern. More important than the cosmetic differences, however, are the different styles of plumbing and operation. Low-level toilets, where cistern and pan are connected by a short length of pipe, are one of the most common forms. Close-coupled toilets do away with the connecting pipe altogether, with cistern and pan incorporated into one construction. Back-to-wall models contain all outlet pipework within the shape of the toilet, while the cistern is hidden behind panelling for a neat and streamlined look. Wall-hung toilets are similarly compact but are mounted on concealed brackets, leaving the floor space below completely clear. High-level cisterns, set high on the wall above the toilet and worked by means of a pull-chain, look particularly good in traditional-style bathrooms.

Toilets usually operate on the 'wash down' principle, whereby waste is carried away by water flushed around the rim of the bowl. Also available are quiet and efficient syphonic flushes which draw down the water rather than pouring it in. Conventional waste pipes are bulky, some 10cm (4in) in diameter, and can be a problem to fit, especially in a small space. A useful solution is to choose a toilet fitted with a macerator which shreds waste on flushing and pumps it through a small bore pipe, about 2.5cm (1in) in diameter. This pipe, unlike normal waste pipes which rely on gravity to bear matter away, can run horizontally and therefore allows the installation of a toilet almost anywhere in the house.

Bidets can be either floor-standing or wall-hung and operate on two different principles: either the bidet fills in the same way as a basin (over the rim, from conventional or mixer taps), or it fills from beneath the rim and often includes a spray option. Consult an expert before buying a bidet or toilet to ensure that your chosen model is suitable for your house and conforms to local water regulations.

Plumbing guidelines usually recommend that the bidet is sited as near as possible to the toilet and the two sit side by side in this cool, all-white bathroom (above). Positioning toilet, bidet and, if possible, bath and basin in a line is most cost-effective, allowing for one straight run of water pipes. Here, matching fixtures, together with co-ordinating taps, mixer spouts and shower fittings, give the room a strong sense of unity. Spray from the shower attachment would fall within the confines of the capacious corner bath, so there is little need for a shower screen, especially as walls and floor are tiled throughout. Downlighters wash the walls with light and efficient ventilation has been installed to compensate for the lack of windows.

BASINS

Most basins, together with toilets and bidets, are made of vitreous china. They come in a vast array of sizes and designs and can be white or coloured, but do be wary about choosing darker tones for these bathroom fixtures: they show up any hard-water scale and soap deposits much more clearly than white or pastel colours.

Basins can either be supported on pedestals and secured against the wall, or be wall-hung. The former allows pipework to be concealed and is often the more decorative option, as the design of the pedestal usually complements the other fittings in the suite. The pedestal also provides a stronger base if, for example, the basin is going to be used for washing clothes. Wall-hung basins free up space below and can look neat and streamlined,

particularly if pipework is concealed in a half-pedestal. They also leave the floor uncluttered for ease of cleaning. A third option is a counter-top basin, which can be sunk into or under a work surface and can be combined with built-in storage underneath. If space is limited and the design of the basin permits, mounting taps on the wall above will free up more of the basin shelf for toiletries.

Some counter-top basins have a pronounced rim designed to sit over the work surface, ensuring a watertight seal. Others are specially designed with no rim at all and are intended to sit under the work surface; in this situation, it is vital that the work surface extends far enough over the edge of the basin to prevent leaks but not so far that there is an overhang which will harbour dirt and germs.

BEFORE YOU BUY:

- Go to bathroom showrooms and try out fittings for size as well as style.
- If starting from scratch, choose fittings that complement each other; basins, toilets and bidets come in matching suites and you will need to select an appropriate bath.
- If you are trying to coordinate old fittings, beware the different shades of 'white' available. They range from pale grey through to almost-cream and finding a perfect match can be difficult.
- White bathroom fittings are timeless classics; darker colours tend to date quickly and have the added disadvantage of making soap stains even more obvious.
- Don't forget to budget for essential 'extras' such as taps and plugs for basins and baths, and levers and seats for toilets.
- Ensure that a shower is suitable for your home before you buy. The position of the water tanks, the water pressure and the existing plumbing will all affect your choice.
- Work out your storage requirements at the outset rather than as an afterthought; they may have a bearing on the fittings you choose.

STORAGE

Storage is a necessary element in most bathrooms and it is a fact of life that however much space is available you will always have too much clutter to fill it. Depending on the size and style of your bathroom, towels, toiletries and other items can either be concealed behind cupboard doors or curtains or left visible on open shelves. A practical combination of the two, with less decorative items such as cleaning fluids and medicines hidden well out of sight and the reach of small children, often proves ideal.

Ready-made storage units include wall-hung cabinets and floor-standing cupboards. Often fitted with a mirrored door and a built-in light fitting and shaver socket, wall-hung units provide useful over-basin storage for toiletries and other everyday items. Floor-standing cupboards are usually designed for use with a specific basin, either one with a decorative upstand or surround in the traditional Edwardian style, or a counter-top basin which can be sunk into a work surface. Also available are standard bathroom shelves in glass, wood or plastic; some have holes designed for toothbrushes, others have small decorative rails to contain the items on display.

Every bathroom is different but some often under-utilized areas include the space below the basin, the wall space above the bath, the area around the hot-water tank (provided it is easily accessible) and around the toilet cistern. Under-basin cupboards (see above) are one space-saving option but a simple and decorative way of creating extra storage here is to hang a gathered frill around the basin. This can be attached to the basin itself by means of Velcro or tacked on to a wooden frame, but either way will cost little in terms of time and money. Wall-hung shelves, corner cupboards and Shaker-style pegs are all ways of utilizing space over the bath in an attractive and practical fashion, while boxing-in the toilet cistern creates an instant shelf. If your hot-water tank is located in the bathroom it may be feasible to install slatted shelves around it, creating the ideal airing/storage cupboard for linen and laundry.

Don't neglect the idea of comfort in the bathroom. A heated towel rail, either run by electricity or connected to the hot-water system, will provide warm, dry towels as well as a modicum of heating, while an armchair, upholstered in soft towelling, or a cushioned window seat provides somewhere to relax.

A PLACE FOR EVERYTHING

The choice of storage is usually dictated by the style and fittings of the bathroom. Recessed into the marble-tiled wall, this mirrored cabinet (left) blends easily with its contemporary surroundings. Inset lighting enhances the coppery tones of the interior as well as illuminating the basin, while the mirrored door conceals the items inside and also serves to reflect daylight into the room. The narrow gap between the basin and the window allows just enough room for a towel rail.

In this attic room (far left, above), the exposed beams set the tone for the chunky travertine worktop and natural linen curtains, tied with tapes, which conceal extensive storage space below. The arrangement of pictures and mirror echoes the slope of the roof, and a high-level towel rack makes use of the often redundant wall space above the bath.

Under-basin storage is given a completely new meaning with this custom-designed cylindrical cabinet (far left, below). Tapering down from the elegantly curved basin, the doors open to reveal a smart black interior with a chrome and glass shelf.

STORAGE SOLUTIONS

As well as fitting conventional cupboards, assess the potential of any under-used areas such as above the bath or around the basin. A sturdy shelf at cornice level like the one in this all-white bathroom (above right) creates a perfect display area for accessories as well as a neat framework for mirrored panels below.

This basin (below right), set into a simple, mosaic-tiled surround, incorporates an open shelf for towels. The remaining space beneath is filled with wicker baskets with handles which can easily be pulled out and used for storing clean linen or dirty laundry.

Sometimes the simplest measures can serve to increase storage space. Positioning the bath out from the wall rather than up against it (far right) freed up space under the windows to right and left for basins set into cupboards. Their unusual curved design allows easy access to both shelves and bath taps.

SMALL BATHROOMS

With a little planning and careful measuring, a bathroom can be created out of a remarkably compact space. Whether it involves new use of an attic or other previously redundant area or whether it is a case of carving the space out of an existing room, it is often surprising just how little is needed to create that invaluable extra bathroom. Specially designed fittings, devices such as under-basin cupboards and clever use of mirror and lighting can all make the most of the smallest space.

Mirror plays both a decorative and a functional role in small bathrooms, acting to make the room look larger and as an effective, waterproof splashback.

In this attic bathroom (previous page, left) a triangular mirrored panel makes a feature of the dividing wall between shelves and basins. Conventional vertical mirrors above the basins were impossible to fit due to the sloping ceiling, and the panel plays a practical role, visually extending the chunky pine work surface. Note how effective the simple, modular shelving becomes when filled with an array of well-chosen and imaginatively displayed accessories.

Lining opposite sides of a room with mirror creates reflections 'ad infinitum'. The entire basin corner in this bathroom (previous page, right) has been mirrored, allowing plenty of 'viewing' space as well as bouncing light back from the mirror on the opposite wall and from the window.

SAVING SPACE

As space is at a premium when planning a small bathroom, be ruthless about what you need. List out the essentials: do you need a bath and a shower or could you survive with just one or the other? Is a bidet absolutely vital? Can you make do with a small corner basin rather than a full-size one? Plot out the fittings on a piece of graph paper (see page 12) and take into account the space required between them, particularly if the room is to be used by more than one person.

The small bathroom is a fact of modern life and there are numerous space-saving fittings and fixtures on the market. Compact plunge baths compensate for lack of

DECORATIVE DETAIL

Even the smallest bathroom can be given character and charm with decorative objects and accessories, but it can require imagination and ingenuity to display them. In this tiny bathroom (far left), space is limited and the toilet is positioned right up against the bath. With little room for conventional shelving, the toilet cistern provides a display area for a brass sailing ship. There are other space-saving measures at work here: the large, framed mirror has the effect of making the bath alcove appear larger, and the slatted wooden blind is a more appropriate window treatment for a small room than a festooned curtain.

Sky-blue panelling, running horizontally to resemble the hull of a boat, provides a high-level shelf for a collection of starfish (left). Often under-utilized, the picture-rail (plate-rail) area of the wall provides a safe haven for bathroom ornaments, well out of splashing range, and here the angled points of the starfish lend a deceptive feeling of height to the room and draw the eye up towards the decorative arch of the window. White porcelain bottles are neatly graded by size on a decorative hanging shelf and the starfish motif reappears in white above the basin.

ATTIC LIFE

Attic conversions do not usually require planning permission, though you should consult an expert if you plan to make changes to the exterior, such as fitting new windows. If the attic space is to include a bathroom, take advice from an experienced plumber before you begin.

This bathroom (right) has been carved out of the roof space, and the ceiling on one side slopes steeply to the floor. Blocking off the lowest section with a false wall (see cross-section) allowed the toilet cistern and pipework to be hidden and also left space for storage. The bath fits across the room, one end almost touching the sloping ceiling but, with taps fitted on one of the long sides rather than the end, the bather can stretch out in comfort. The door opens outwards but a sliding door could be fitted if space is at a premium.

Two dormer windows flood this attic bathroom (far right) with daylight and the all-white scheme makes the space look bright and airy rather than cramped. All-over splashproof tiling negates any need for a shower cubicle and the shower, fitting neatly under the peak of the roof, is open-plan with the rest of the room. An extractor fan fitted into the sloping ceiling provides extra ventilation.

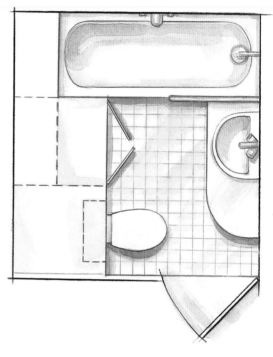

length by extra depth, allowing the bather to enjoy a relaxing soak despite restrictions of space. A corner bath can be useful, fitting more easily into certain rooms than a conventional rectangular bath. Taps can be wall-mounted or fitted to one side of the bath, allowing the bather a little extra room to stretch out.

Installing a shower over the bath is one space-saving measure, but self-contained, freestanding shower units take up less space than you might think and can be fitted either within the bathroom or elsewhere in the house.

Supplied with four panels and sometimes a roof as well to keep in steam and reduce condensation, they are completely watertight and do not rely on existing walls for support. Provided that plumbing and ventilation requirements can be met, they can be fitted into spaces such as under-stair cupboards or hallways as well as into bedrooms or one-room apartments.

Wall-hung basins are ideal for smaller bathrooms. Available in all shapes and sizes, including tiny corner models for hand-washing, they free up valuable floor

- Keep fittings to a minimum and consider space-savers such as wall-hung basins and 'back-to-wall' toilets.
- Design access to the bathroom to take up as little room space as possible: hang the door to open outwards, or fit a sliding door or two half-doors.
- Maximize storage to minimize clutter, using wasted empty space such as the area under the basin.
- Keep to a one- or two-colour scheme, continuing it through from walls and tiles to towels and accessories.
- Long, lined curtains can be bulky. Substitute unlined voile or muslin, or a Roman or roller blind.
- Visually 'open out' the space with mirrored panels and/or framed mirrors.
- Utilize areas such as boxed-in cisterns and picture-rails (plate-rails) to display decorative accessories.
- Accent your decorative scheme with well-planned lighting inset into the ceiling and/or set above the basin.
- Scale up rather than down: large pictures or objects make a room look more spacious, while costly materials such as marble, polished wood and brass are more affordable in small quantities and add a touch of luxury.

space. Alternatively, counter-top basins set into cupboards allow for valuable extra storage space beneath and on the worktop itself. Streamlined modern mixer taps are compact alternatives to traditional taps and leave more room on the basin shelf for soaps, bottles, toothbrushes and so on.

'Back-to-wall' toilets and bidets, in which pipework is hidden within the unit, have a neat finish, while wall-hung versions free up floor space and are particularly compact, especially if the cistern is boxed in or hidden behind a panelled wall. A standard toilet requires an area of about

140cm x 70cm (55in x 28in) for comfortable use but new slimline cisterns can reduce this. If the room is high enough, an old-fashioned high-level cistern fixed to the wall above the toilet is a good space-saving alternative, as the toilet pan can sit against the wall beneath it rather than projecting forward from the cistern, as it does in more modern designs.

One of the main obstacles to installing a new bathroom, whether large or small, is often the plumbing for the toilet. As discussed in the previous chapter, toilet

CURVES AND CONTOURS

Unusually shaped rooms call for unusually shaped baths. If you think you have insufficient space for a tub it is worth investigating the variations on the standard rectangular theme. Curved and contoured baths mean fewer hard angles, allowing for easier passage in a restricted space; corner baths can provide a full-length tub in rooms where a normal rectangle might not fit; small, square plunge baths take up minimal space, as well as conveniently doubling up as shower areas.

In this triangular bathroom (right), a contoured bath has been fitted into the narrowest angle of the room, with pipework for both shower and taps neatly concealed. The mosaic-tiled floor is stepped up around the bath, accentuating its curves and creating a splashproof surround. A clear glass panel screens the shower. Despite the size and shape of the room, there is still space left over for double basins, wall-hung to leave the floor clear, and a row of spacious cupboards above. The streamlined mixer taps are a compact option for small basins, leaving more space to either side for soap, toothbrushes, and so on.

waste pipes are bulky and sometimes awkward to connect, especially in small spaces; consult an architect or plumber first. One possible solution is a toilet fitted with a macerator (waste shredder). These require only a narrow pipe, which can be run horizontally rather than on a gradient and fits more easily behind walls. If the bathroom is close to or en suite to the bedroom, ask to hear the macerator in action before buying; they can be disconcertingly noisy, especially in the middle of the night.

Awkward corners

If your bathroom is an unconventional shape, use all the space available to the full. An L-shaped room might provide the perfect location for a shower cubicle to be tucked away in the shorter branch of the 'L'. A square room, on the

other hand, would lend itself better to a small bath with a shower head over it, screened with a curtain or panel. An awkwardly steep, sloping ceiling in an attic room can be turned to your advantage: screen off the lowest area with a false wall and use it for storage or to conceal pipework and cistern for the toilet and bidet; the higher-ceilinged level is then free for a bath and/or shower. Rethink the access to the room: a full-size door can take up valuable space if it opens inwards and two half-doors or a sliding door might be more appropriate. Sometimes simply rehanging the door to open outwards can make all the difference. Utilize any recesses or other nooks and crannies: the most unlikely spaces can be used for storage, either for everyday items or for decorative accessories that will lend your bathroom character and charm.

Decoration

Decoration can play an important part in the small bathroom. A monochrome or near-monochrome colour scheme makes for an unfussy, uncluttered look, especially if carried through to towels and other accessories. A small room can be ill-proportioned; draw an imaginary line around the walls at dado- or chair-rail height and paint them a darker shade below and a lighter shade above to give a feeling of height. Conversely, darkening the ceiling will draw down an over-high room.

Finally, do not be afraid to scale up. A large picture or a bold sculpture can give a cramped room an unexpected feeling of space, whereas smaller items may simply accentuate the lack of it. Use mirrored panels or framed mirrors to visually enlarge a room and install good lighting to brighten the whole scheme.

ANGLES AND DIAGONALS

Space is very restricted in this sunny
yellow, top-lit bathroom (left) but there
is still room for a full-sized bath and
basin. Even with the bathroom mapped
out on graph paper, the owners might
have thought twice before placing the
bath and basin so close together but,
thanks to the unusual angles of the bath,
there is just enough space both to use
the basin and to pass between it and the
bath to reach the toilet. The toilet itself
is a neat, compact 'back-to-wall' design,
with the cistern and pipework hidden
behind the tiled wall. Panels of mirror
above the basin and triangular shelf and
at the far end of the bath 'open out' the
space, while the tiling has been
imaginatively designed: not only does
the smart black-and-white border add a
dramatic note but the minuscule floor
space has been tiled diagonally, echoing
the angles of the room and creating a
deceptive feeling of space. The black
bath handle and black-and-white towel
radiator pick up the theme of the border
and even towels and soap are fully
colour-coordinated.

INDEX

PUBLISHER'S ACKNOWLEDGMENTS

Conran Octopus would like to thank the following photographers and organizations for their permission to reproduce the photographs in this book:

1-3 photograph: Simon Kenny (designer: Danny Venlet)/Belle; 4-5 Jerome Darblay; 6 Deidi von Schaewen; 8-9 Alexander van Berge; 9 Bernard Toillon/S.I.P./Elizabeth Whiting & Associates; 10 Hoetze Eisma/V.T. Wonen; 13 Hoetze Eisma/V.T. Wonen; 14-15 Russell Brooks/Australian House & Garden Design; 16 Marianne Haas/Elle Decoration/Scoop; 17 Verne Fotografie; 18 Rodney Hyett/Australian House & Garden Design; 19 photograph: Roland Beaufre (chateau Smith Haut-Lafitte)/Agence Top; 20 photographer: Alexandre Bailhache (stylist: Catherine Ardouin)/Marie Claire Maison; 21 Spike Powell/Judi Goodwin/ Elizabeth Whiting & Associates; 22 Richard Davies (architect: John Pawson); 23 Chris Drake/Homes and Gardens/Robert Harding Syndication; 24-25 Deidi von Schwaen; 25 Elizabeth Whiting & Associates; 26 James Mortimer/The Interior Archive; 27 Tim Beddow (designers: Craig Hamilton & Tina Joyce); 28-29 'Colourwash'; 28 left: Fritz von der Schulenburg/The Interior Archive; 30 Rodney Hyett/ Australian House & Garden Design; 31 left Tim Beddow; 31 right: Hotze Eisma; 32-33 Tim Goffe courtesy of House & Garden; 34-35 Verne Fotografie; 35 Jean Pierre Godeaut; 36-37 Jacques Dirand; 37 Tim Goffe/Conran Octopus; 38 above: Trevor Richards/Homes & Gardens/Robert Harding Syndication; 38 below: Simon Wheeler; 39 Paul Ryan/International Interiors; 40 photograph: Peter Rad (designer: Nicola McGaan)/Belle; 41 Hotze Eisma; 42 right: Nadia Mackenzie/Elizabeth Whiting & Associates; 42 left: Weidenfeld Nicolson Archive; 43 photograph: Pascal Chevallier (designer: MichelKlein)/Agence Top; 44 Abitare; 45 Marianne Haas/Elle Decoration/Scoop; 46-47 Hotze Eisma; 47 right: photograph: Gilles de Chabaneix (stylist: Rozensztroch)/Marie Claire Maison; 48 right: Jacques Dirand (designer: Gordon Watson); 48 left: photograph: Nicolas Tosi (stylist: Marion Bayle)/Marie Claire Maison; 49 Henry Bourne/Elle Decoration; 50 left: David Parmiter; 50 right: V.T. Wonen; 51 below: Polly Wreford/Country Homes & Interiors/Robert Harding Syndication; 51 above: Hoetze Eisma/V.T. Wonen; 52 left: photograph: Nicolas Tosi (stylist: Julie Borgeaud)/Marie Claire Maison; 52 right: Paul Warchol; 53 right: photograph: Neil Lorimer (architect: Andrew Norbury)/Belle; 53 left Wulf Brackrock; 54-55 Dennis Gilbert (designer: Rick Mather); right: John Hall; 56 Jan Baldwin; 57 Claudio Silvestrin; 58 Richard Bryant/Arcaid; 59 right: Reiner Blunck (designer: Geoffrey Pie); 59 left: James Mortimer/The Interior Archive; 60 left: photograph: Neil Lorimer (architect: Andrew Norbury)/Belle; 60-61 Hoetze Eisma/V.T. Wonen; 61 right: Fritz von der Schulenburg/Country Homes & Interiors/Robert Harding Picture Syndication; 62 Alexander van Berge; 63 right: Russell Brook/Australian House & Garden Design; 63 left: Gilles de Chabaneix/Elle Decoration/Scoop; 64 left: photograph: Simon Kenny (designer: Chris Hosking)/Belle; 64 right: Marianne Majerus (designer: Barbara Weiss); 65 John Hall; 66 below: Marzia Chierichetti - Fabrizio Bergamo/Elle Decor Italy; 66 above: Marianne Haas/Elle Decoration/Scoop; 67 Paul Warchol; 68 below left: Bernard Touillon/S.I.P./Elizabeth Whiting & Associates; 68 top left: Jan Baldwin/Homes & Gardens/Robert Harding Picture Syndication; 68-69 Guillaume De Laubier/Elle Decoration/Scoop; 70-71 Hotze Eisma; 71 John Hall; 72 Simon Brown; 73 Jerome Darblay; 75 Jacques Dirand (designer: Compain); 76 Richard Davies/Future Systems; 78 Schoner Wohnen/Camera Press

AUTHOR'S ACKNOWLEDGMENTS

I would like to extend my warmest thanks to the team at Conran Octopus for their help and encouragement, which made this project both enjoyable and remarkably stress-free. I would also like to thank my husband and my children, who still find it highly amusing that anyone could actually write a whole book about bathrooms.